GIFTED & TALENTED

To develop your child's gifts and talents

READING

Written by Tracy Masonis

McGraw Hill Children's Publishing

Columbus, Ohio

Dear Parents,

Gifted & Talented Reading has been designed specifically to promote the development of analytic thinking and higher-level language development skills. The activities in this book use a variety of critical reading strategies to derive and interpret meaning. All of the activities will spark your child's imagination, inspire creativity, and foster a love of reading.

The activities are intended to reinforce and extend the reading concepts your child has already been introduced to at school or at home. For example, the character, setting, and events activities step beyond simply identifying these concepts; they motivate your child to brainstorm original examples independently. Most of the activities can be completed directly on the workbook pages. In some instances, though, your child might prefer to use a separate sheet of paper to interpret what has been read.

While working in this book, your child may be inspired to create his or her own reading activities. If so, have your child read them aloud and explain the strategies to you. Praise your child's efforts, and encourage him or her to continue creating them. This type of activity not only stimulates creativity, but it also deepens your child's love of reading and appreciation of language development.

McGraw-Hill Children's Publishing

Send all inquiries to:
McGraw-Hill Children's Publishing
8787 Orion Place
Columbus, OH 43240-4027

ISBN 1-57768-981-X

1 2 3 4 5 6 7 8 9 10 VHG 07 06 05 04 03 02

The McGraw-Hill Companies

Table of Contents

Knowing the Words/Vocabulary/Language Development

Elements of Stories

Reading Comprehension

We're the Same!

Words that mean the **same** thing, or close to the same thing, are called **synonyms**.

Write a word from the Word List that has the same meaning as each word below.

Word List			
bright	hop	dad	fast
pretty	plate	silly	center

sunny

____

beautiful

____

middle

____

dish

____

quick

____

jump

____

goofy

____

father

____

Name ____________________________

Synonym Squares!

Circle the **synonym** in each square that has the same meaning or close to the same meaning as the word in **bold** print.

end	**start**
begin (circled)	
stop	

scream	**shout**
brother	
talk	

cat	**sick**
bath	
ill	

Think of a synonym for each of the three listed words. Then write a sentence using **both** words in your sentence.

smart/____________________

____

____

bad/____________________

____

____

little/____________________

____

____

Take My Place

Name ______________________________

Choose the word from the Word List below that could take the place of the underlined word in each sentence. Write it on the line.

Word List

pick	tired	cut
porch	pull	bag

I was so sleepy! I couldn't wait to go to bed! ______________________________

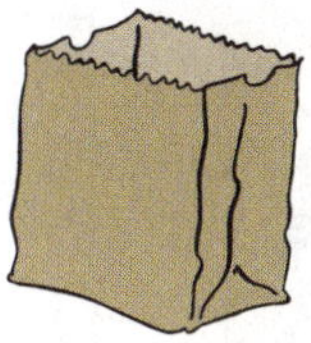

Please put all your books in this sack.

____

Please choose a present you would like to open. ______________________________

Are you strong enough to drag this heavy crate? ______________________________

"It is important to trim the extra fabric on your art project," said my art teacher.

____

We sipped lemonade on the deck.

____

Name ______________________________

Antonym Artists!

Antonyms are words that have **opposite** meanings. Abby and Abe are Antonym Artists! They like to draw opposite pictures. Help Abe draw the opposite of Abby's pictures.

Name ______________________

Oops! It's Opposite Day!

Oppie woke up early one morning to discover it was Opposite Day! Everything was opposite! Oppie got dressed, and all his clothes went on backwards! Help Oppie by circling the word in each row that has the opposite meaning of the first word.

pull	push	pillow	grab
fast	burger	danger	slow
thin	fat	tall	skinny
break	fix	hold	glue
harm	ham	cold	help
winter	february	summer	fall
loser	bad	teacher	winner

Name ______________________

Antonyms Are Opposites!

Words with **opposite** meanings are called **antonyms**. Circle an antonym for the underlined word in each sentence.

The sky was very dark.	purple	old	light
Turn left at the light.	right	sideways	yellow
The shelf was very high.	pretty	low	loud
The turtle walked slowly.	silly	quickly	nicely
I whispered at the circus.	laughed	coughed	shouted
Bobby is an adult.	child	fan	principal
The clown was very strong.	weak	silly	hungry
The library is a quiet place.	fun	messy	noisy

Batty Bats!

Some words have more than one meaning.

The word *bat* has more than one meaning.

Look at the words and their meanings below. Next to each picture, write the letter that has the correct meaning.

can: A) a metal container
B) to know how

____  ____ 

band: A) a group of musicians
B) a strip of material

____  ____ 

cap: A) a soft hat with a visor
B) lid or cover

____ 

____ 

crow: A) a large black bird
B) the loud cry of a rooster

____  ____ 

Name ____________________

Match That Meaning!

Some words have more than one meaning. Look at the list of words. Match the word's correct meaning to the pictures below.

cross: A) to draw a line through
B) angry

fall: C) the season between summer and winter
D) to trip or stumble

land: E) to bring to a stop or rest
F) the ground

____

____

____

____

____

____

Name ____________________

Match That Meaning!

The word *may* has more than one meaning.

May or **may:** A) the fifth month of the year
B) to be permitted or allowed to do something

MAY						
Sunday	Monday	Tuesday	Wednesday	Thursday	Friday	Saturday
			1	2	3	4
5	6	7	8	9	10	11
12	13	14	15	16	17	18
19	20	21	22	23	24	25
26	27	28	29	30	31	

Write the letter of the correct meaning in each blank.

My dad's birthday is in __________.

__________ I please go to the gym?

Many flowers bloom in __________.

Mother, __________ I go to the swimming party?

My brother will come home from college in __________.

Name ______________________________

Common Corrections

Some words look and sound very much alike, but have very different meanings. For example, make sure you ask for an extra piece of *dessert*, not *desert*!

dessert

desert

Look at the words and meanings below.
Write the correct word to complete each sentence.

quiet: not noisy
quite: very

Shhhh, please be ____________________ in the library.

The turkey was ____________________ good.

freight: cargo
fright: sudden fear

The ship carried a lot of ____________________.

The loud noise gave me a sudden ____________________.

lose: misplace
loose: not tight

My front tooth was ____________________.

Did you ____________________ your homework?

Name ____________________

Common Corrections

Some words look and sound very much alike, but have very different meanings. Look at the words and meanings below. Write the correct word to complete each sentence.

couch: a sofa
coach: someone who trains athletes

I fell asleep on the ____________________.

The ____________________ gave the football team a pep talk.

picture: a visual representation
pitcher: a container for liquids

We hung the ____________________ in the kitchen.

"Please pass the ____________________ lemonade," I said.

guessed: made a guess
guest: visitor

I was a ____________________ in their house.

He ____________________ the answer and got it right!

Name ______________________________

Caitlin Uses Context Clues

When you read, it is important to know about context clues. **Context clues** can help you figure out the meaning of a word or a missing word just by looking at the **other words** in the sentence.

Read each sentence below. Circle the context clues, or other words in the sentence that give you hints about the meaning. Choose the answer that fits in each blank. Write it on the line.

It was so hot outside that I decided I would go to the beach and ____swim____.

A) play B) laugh C) shovel D) swim

D) is the correct answer because of the context clues hot and beach. Now you try.

Last night I went to bed very late and now I feel ______________.

A) happy B) hungry C) tired D) yawn

When I broke my mom's favorite vase she was ______________.

A) worried B) nice C) magic D) angry

The clown looked very ______________ wearing a tiny pink tutu!

A) silly B) smart C) orange D) light

Name ______________________________

Caitlin Uses More Context Clues

When you read, it is important to know about context clues. **Context clues** can help you figure out the missing word in a sentence, just by looking at the **other words** in the sentence.

Read each sentence below. Circle the context clues. Choose the answer that fits in each blank. Write it on the line.

The cold wind and lack of heat made me wish I had an extra ____________________.

A) umbrella B) toy C) shovel D) jacket

A whale is a very ____________________ mammal. Sailors often thought whales were actually small islands!

A) small B) graceful C) large D) blue

Eating fruit is important for ____________________ health. Fruit is full of many important vitamins.

A) bad B) good C) okay D) cat

The bus was very large and had a lot of seats. It could carry ____________________ people.

A) few B) hungry C) many D) tired

Name ______________________________

Carlo's Context Clues

Context clues can help you figure out the meaning of a word just by looking at the **other words** in the sentence.

Read each sentence below. Circle the context clues. Choose a word from the Word List to replace each word in **bold**. Write it on the line.

Word List

stop	shined	tease
smart	lively	yummy

This prize-winning chocolate cream pie is **delicious**. ______________________

Please do not **taunt** your younger brother. Mean words hurt his feelings. ______________________

The police officer told us to **halt** when we came to the red traffic light. ______________________

The bouncy, happy puppy was very **energetic**. ______________________

The silver bowl really **gleamed** after you polished it. ______________________

The **intelligent** girl always got 100's on her spelling tests. ______________________

Name ______________________

Carlo's Context Clues Continued

Context clues can help you figure out the meaning of a word just by looking at the **other words** in the sentence.

Read each sentence below. Circle the context clues. Choose a word from the Word List to replace each word in **bold**. Write it on the line.

Word List

petted	understand	tell
little	yelled	

"Don't **reveal** the secret! We want the party to be a surprise!" said Mary. ______________________

I can't **grasp** that hard math problem! It is too difficult. ______________________

The baby bird was so **tiny** that we could hardly see it. ______________________

We **stroked** the soft kitten and heard it purr. ______________________

The crowd **hollered** when the player was called out. ______________________

What Is a Character?

Name ______________________________

A **character** is the **person**, **animal**, or **object** that a story is about. You can't have a story without a character.

Characters are usually people, but sometimes they can be animals, aliens (!), or even objects that come to life. You can have many characters in a story.

Read the story below and then answer the questions about the main character on the next page.

Jumpin' Jack!

Everybody liked Jumpin' Jack. He was the nicest rabbit in the forest. If he found a carrot, he would split it in half and share it with you. If the baby bunnies were having trouble with their jumps, Jumpin' Jack would patiently help them practice.

Jumpin' Jack had two pointy white ears, a black body, and four white feet that looked like socks. He was very handsome!

The End

Name ______________________________

Character Continued

First, authors must decide who their main character is going to be. Next, they must decide what their main character looks like. Then, they reveal their character's personality by **what** their character does.

Who is the main character in "Jumpin' Jack!"?

____

What does Jumpin' Jack look like? Describe his appearance.

____

____

Give two examples of what Jumpin' Jack **does** that show that he is kind: ______________________________

____

____

Would you want Jumpin' Jack as a friend? Why or why not?

____

____

____

Name ______________________________

Character Interview—Lights! Camera! Action!

An **interview** takes place between two people, usually a reporter and another person. The interviewer asks questions for the person to answer.

Pretend that you are a reporter. Choose a character from a book you read. If you could ask the character anything you wanted to, what would you ask?

Make a **list of questions** you would like to ask your character:

1. ______________________________
2. ______________________________
3. ______________________________
4. ______________________________

Now pretend your character has come to life and could **answer your questions**. Write what you think he, she, or it would say:

1. ______________________________
2. ______________________________
3. ______________________________
4. ______________________________

Name ___________________________

Setting—Place

Every story has a **setting**. The setting is the **place** where the story happens. Think of a place that you know well. It could be your room, your kitchen, your backyard, your classroom, or an imaginary place.

Brainstorm some words and ideas about that place. Think about what you see, hear, smell, taste, or feel in that place.

Brainstorm your ideas for a setting below:

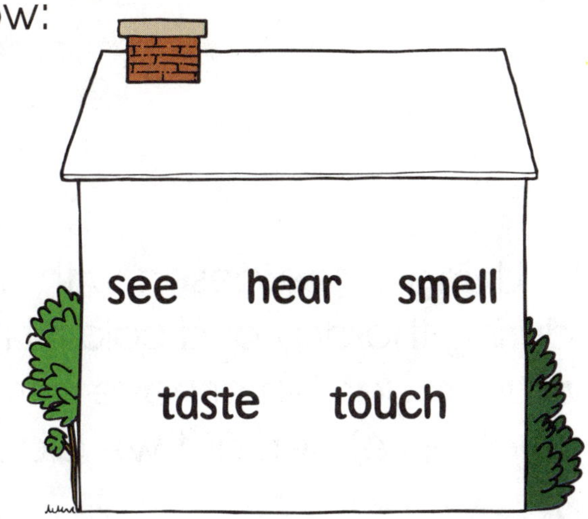

____

____

____

____

____

____

____

____

____

____

____

Where are we? ___________________________

Name ____________________

Setting—Place

Read the story below and answer the questions about the setting.

Desert Life

Living in the desert with my family wasn't easy. It was very hot during the day and cold at night. The ground was so dry we couldn't plant a garden or have a front yard with grass. We didn't have trees to climb either, but we did have lots of cacti!

What is the temperature like in the desert? ____________________

If you were going to visit the desert, what clothes would you take?

____

____

Could you plant a garden in the desert? Why or why not?

____

____

Are there trees for kids to climb in the desert? ____________________

Setting—Time

The **setting** is the **place** where the story happens. The setting is also the **time** in which the story happens. A reader needs to know **when** the story is happening. Does it take place at night? On a sunny day? In the future? During the winter?

Time can be:

time of day

a holiday

a season of the year

a time in history

a time in the future

Read the following story. Then answer the questions below.

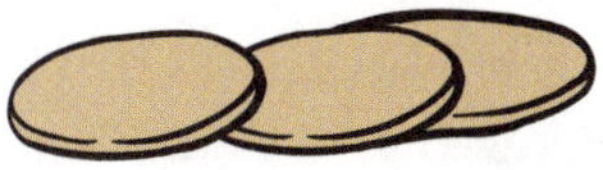

Pancake Mornings

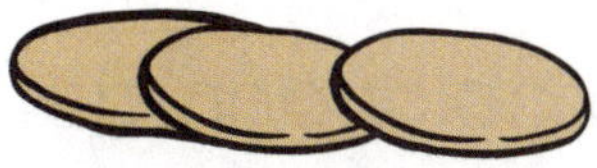

In the summer, I look forward to Sunday mornings. On Sundays, my parents get up extra early. My mom mixes pancake batter with ripe blueberries, and my dad plays the fiddle. When my brother and I come downstairs for breakfast, the pancakes are on the griddle and my dad is dancing!

On what day of the week does this story take place?

____

What season is it in this story? ____________________

What time of day is it? ____________________

Make a Map!

Name ____________________

In a story or book you read, the character or characters may have taken a journey or simply walked around their town. Where did the main events in the story take place? Create a detailed map showing the place where the characters lived. You may wish to ask an adult for help.

1. Draw the outline of your map on a sheet of paper.
2. Be sure to write the title and the author of the book at the top of the map.
3. Think about what places you want to include on your map and draw them.
4. Label the important places, adding a short sentence about what happened there.
5. Add color and details.
6. Share your map with friends and tell them about the story you read.

Name ____________________

Extra! Extra! Read All About It!

Newspaper reporters have very important jobs. They have to catch a reader's attention and at the same time **tell the facts**.

Newspaper reporters write their stories by answering **who**, **what**, **where**, **when**, **why**, and **how**. Think about a book you just read and answer the questions below.

Who: **Who** is the story about?

____

What: **What** happened to the main character?

____

Where: **Where** does the story take place?

____

When: **When** does the story take place?

____

Why: **Why** do these story events happen?

____

How: **How** do these events happen?

____

Name ______________________________

Extra! Extra! Read All About It!

Use your answers on page 27 to write a newspaper article about the book you read.

BIG CITY TIMES

Title

____

(Write a catchy title for your article)

Name ______________________________

Fiction or Nonfiction?

Some stories are made up and some are true. **Fiction** stories are made up and **nonfiction** stories are true.

Read the passages below. Then write if they are **fiction** or **nonfiction**.

George Washington was the first president of the United States. The city of Washington, D.C., is named after him.

____

Taddy Bear loved honey. He would always go with his mom to the Bargain Bear Grocery Store. She would let him fill up their grocery cart with lots of honey pots!

____

There are fifty states that make up the United States of America. If you put the fifty states in order alphabetically, the first state would be Alabama and the last state would be Wyoming.

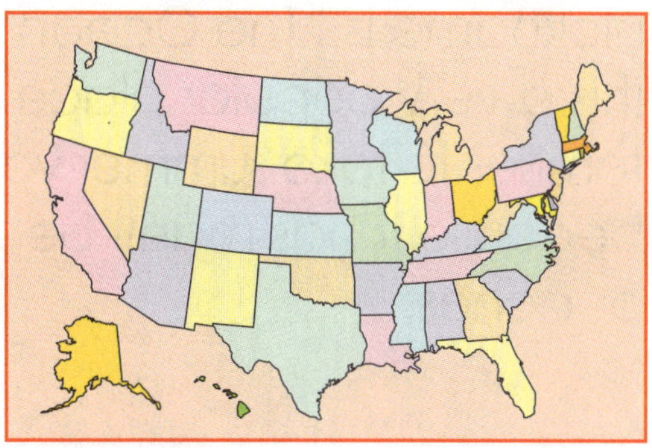

____

Fiction or Nonfiction?

Some stories are made up and some are true. **Fiction** stories are made up and **nonfiction** stories are true.

Read the passages below. Then write if they are **fiction** or **nonfiction**.

Last night, I was invited to Kazam the Magician's house for dinner. I love to visit his house. We always have cotton candy soup and bubble gum soda for dinner. Then we jump into a tub of vanilla ice cream for dessert. I wish dinner was like this at my house!

____

Rhode Island is the smallest state in the United States. Its nickname is "The Ocean State." It is a very popular place for families to take summer vacations because it has many beautiful beaches.

____

Name ______________________

Sequencing Pictures

Put the pictures in each column in order. Write **1**, **2**, or **3** next to each picture.

____

____

____

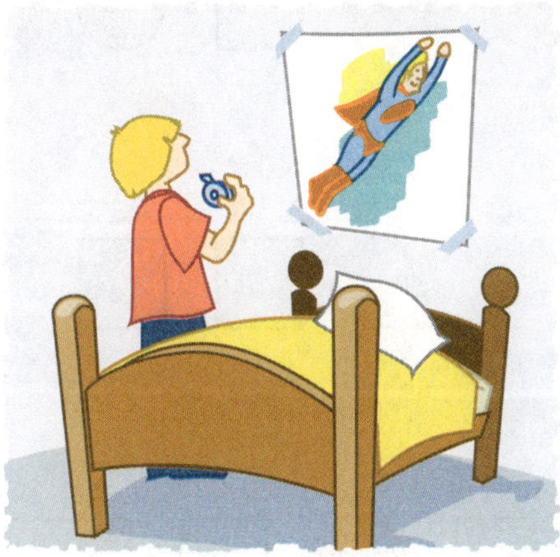

____

____

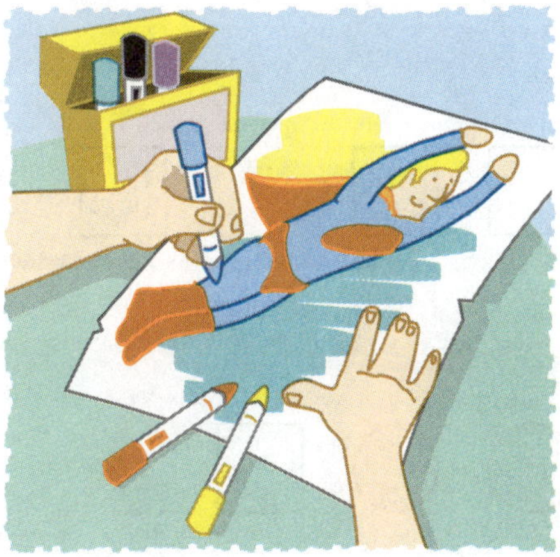

____

Name ____________________

Sequencing Patterns

Look for a pattern of shapes inside each pencil. Choose a shape from the Picture Bank and draw what comes next on each pencil. Then write the name of the shape on the line.

Picture Bank

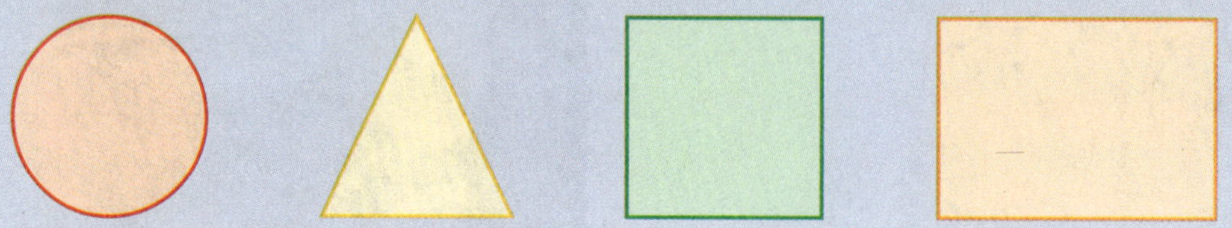

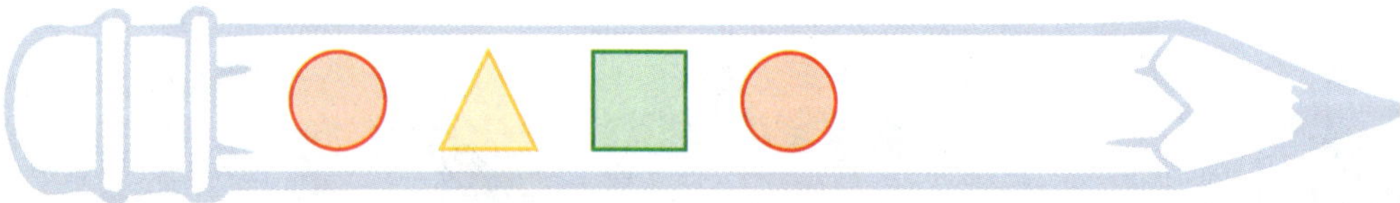

____

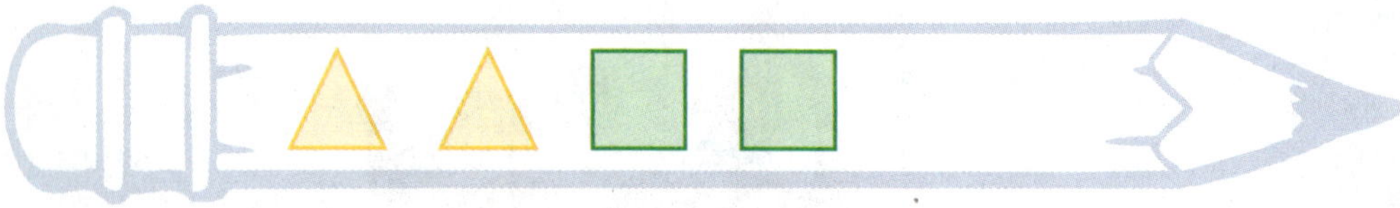

____

____

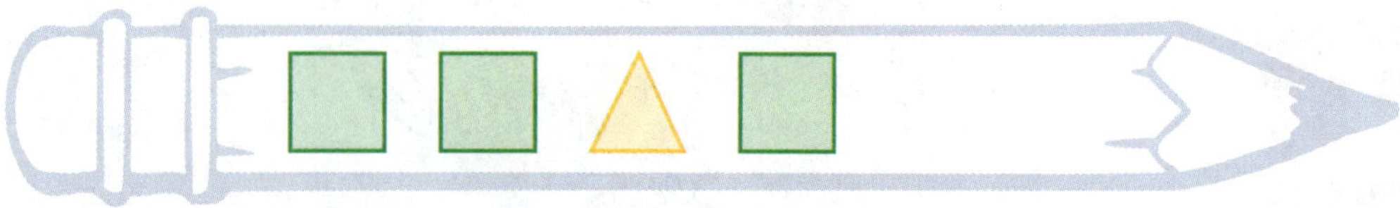

____

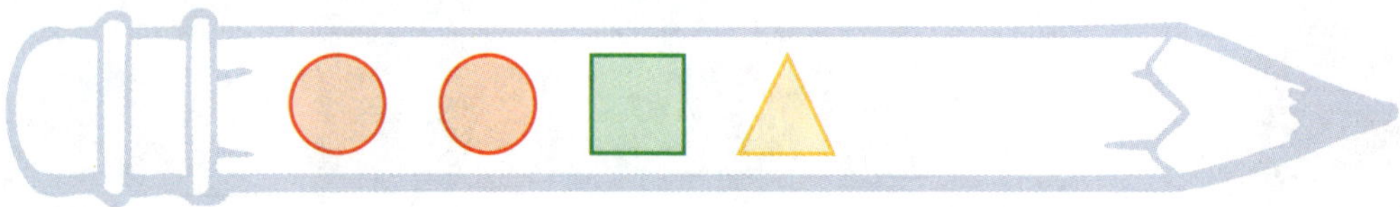

____

Sequencing Riddles

Name ______________________

To solve the riddles below, look at the letter underneath each line. Next, write the letter that comes **before** each letter.

How do you catch a squirrel?

___ ___ ___ ___ ___   ___ ___   ___   ___ ___ ___ ___
D M J N C   V Q   B   U S F F

___ ___ ___   ___ ___ ___   ___ ___ ___ ___   ___   ___ ___ ___.
B O E   B D U   M J L F   B   O V U

What has four wheels and flies?

___   ___ ___ ___ ___ ___ ___ ___
B   H B S C B H F

___ ___ ___ ___ ___
U S V D L

Why did the boy run around his bed?

___ ___   ___ ___ ___ ___ ___   ___ ___   ___ ___
U P   D B U D I   V Q   P O

___ ___ ___   ___ ___ ___ ___ ___
I J T   T M F F Q

Story Time

Name ______________________________

Write each group of sentences in the correct order.

My cat was full and went to sleep. My cat was hungry.
I filled a bowl with cat food.

1. ______________________________
2. ______________________________
3. ______________________________

I got a gold star. I studied for my spelling test.
My teacher gave us a list of spelling words.

1. ______________________________
2. ______________________________
3. ______________________________

Name ______________________________

Hey! What's the Big Idea?

Circle the words that are shown in the picture above.

bowl	spatula	bed	dog	ink
oven	pan	jar	pot	phone
mixer	napkins	scooter	girl	sneakers
mitt	paper towels	car	socks	cupcake tin
spoon		cat	milk	

Circle and write the best title for the picture.

Baking With Dad   Chocolate Attack!   Eating Food

____

Tell why the other two titles are not as good.

____

____

Picture This!

Look at the picture. Circle and write the best title on the lines below.

B-r-r-r, It's Cold! Bears and Birds

Asleep for the Winter Bears Go Shopping

____

____

Fishing Our New Fish

The Pet Store Fish and Chips

____

____

Spring Cleaning My New Toy

Saturday Fun New Shoes

____

____

Picture This!

Write a title beside each picture below. Your title should tell what each picture is about in just a few words.

____

____

____

____

____

____

Name ______________________

What's the Main Idea?

The **main idea** tells about the **whole picture**.

Does the sentence tell the main idea of the picture? Circle *yes* or *no*. Then, write the sentence that best states the main idea for each picture.

The cat wants to play. yes no

The cat takes a nap. yes no

____

____

The brothers play together. yes no

The brothers are smart. yes no

____

____

The dog is hungry. yes no

The dog is playful. yes no

____

____

Name ______________________

Story Time

The **main idea** tells about the **whole story**.

Read the story below.

"Mom, can we build a fort in the dining room?" John asked.

"Sure, honey," said John's mom. Then John's mom covered the dining room table with a giant sheet. "Do you want to eat lunch in our fort?" asked John's mom.

"Yes!" said John. Then John's mom brought two peanut butter sandwiches on paper plates and sat under the table, too!

"Mom, making a fort with you is so much fun!" said John, smiling.

Does the sentence tell the main idea? Write *yes* or *no*.

1. Then John's mom covered the dining room table with a giant sheet. __________
2. "Do you want to eat lunch in our fort?" asked John's mom. __________
3. "Mom, making a fort with you is so much fun!" __________
4. Write a sentence that tells the main idea: __________________

____

Name ____________________

What's Missing?

Circle the object in the second picture that is different from the first picture.

Baseball Daze!

Look at the petals to find the flower that is different. Color the flower that is different.

Petal Power!

Name ____________________

The Pet Shop

Find and circle **ten** things wrong with this picture.

Name ______________________________

Highlight Happy!

Highlighting is a strategy that will help you with your reading. When you highlight something, you use a light-colored marker to color over a special word or words that you want to remember.

Follow the directions to highlight words in the sentences below.

1. Highlight four animals you might see in Alaska.

   In Alaska, you might see bears, whales, sea otters, and moose.

2. Highlight the two things you should take to Alaska if you visit in the summer.

   If you visit Alaska in the summer, you should take bug spray and a raincoat.

3. Highlight three animals that are not from Alaska.

   Flamingos, platypuses, and lions are not from Alaska.

Name ____________________

Sally's Snake

Sally received a new pet snake for her birthday. Sally has a lot to learn about taking care of her new snake. She needs to know how to hold it and clean its cage. She also needs to learn what to feed it. Sally can't wait to learn how to care for her new pet!

What is the **main idea** this story? Circle your choice.

1. Sally had a great birthday.
2. Sally has a lot to learn about caring for her new pet.
3. Sally needs to learn how to hold a snake.

What is **one thing** Sally needs to learn about her new pet?

1. How to clean its cage
2. How to take pictures
3. How to read to her snake

What Is Cause and Effect?

Name ______________________________

Cause: An action or act that makes something happen.

Effect: Something that happens because of an action or cause.

Look at the following example of cause and effect.

Kyle has a spelling test and studies hard.

Kyle's hard work helps him do a super job!

Now draw a line connecting each cause on the left side of the page to its effect on the right side of the page.

Name ______________________________

More Cause and Effect!

Cause: An action or act that makes something happen.

Effect: Something that happens because of an action or cause.

Look at the following example of cause and effect.

Now draw a line connecting each cause on the left side of the page to its effect on the right side of the page.

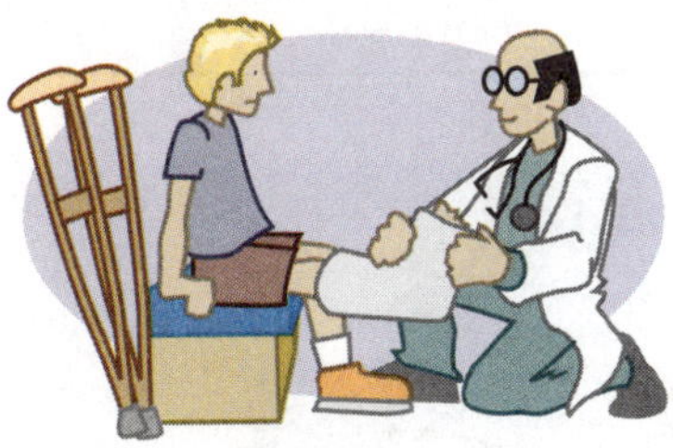

We Go Together!

Name ______________________

Draw a line connecting the pictures that go together. Then figure out which picture is the cause and which is the effect. Write **C** for **cause** or **E** for **effect** under each picture.

____

____

____

____

____

____

What Happened?

Name ____________________

Read the stories below. Then write the missing effect.

Erin and her mom cleaned out their messy garage. Now they have room inside the garage to store Erin's bike.

Cause: Erin and her mom cleaned their messy garage.

What was the effect? ____________________

Frank tried out for the town basketball team and played very well. The next day, he found out that he had made the team.

Cause: Frank tried out for the town basketball team and played very well.

What was the effect? ____________________

Inside Out!

Name ____________________________

Can you match the outsides with the insides? Draw a line from each picture on the left to its inside picture on the right.

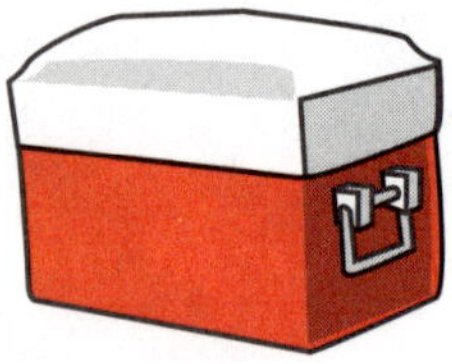

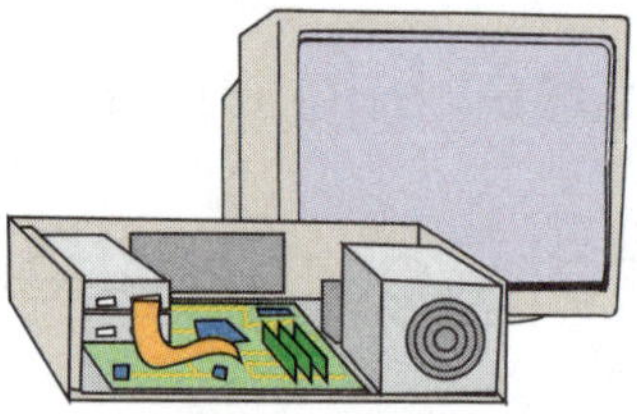

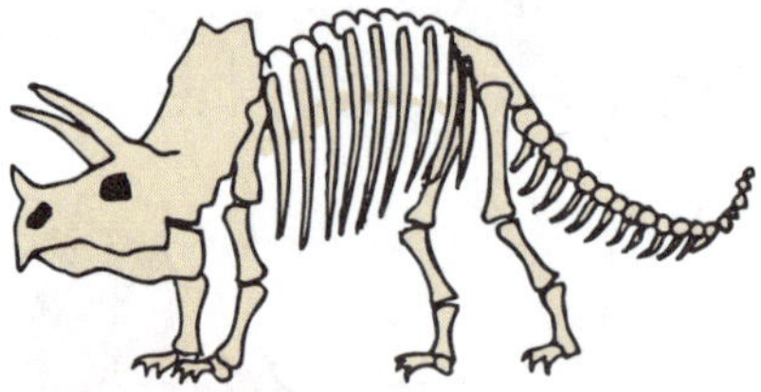

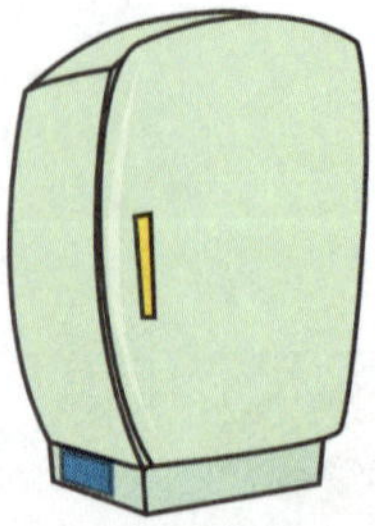

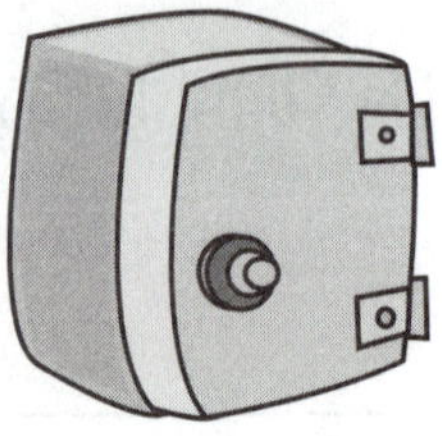

Name ________________________________

Books for Gabby!

Gabby loves to read books about many different topics. She loves to read about exotic animals. She loves stories about famous people. Gabby is also interested in becoming a doctor or an actress one day.

Look at the books below. Circle only the books that Gabby would like to read.

Use Your Head!

Name ________________________________

Read each sentence below. Then read each statement that follows it. Using the information in the first sentence, decide which word best completes each statement. Then write that word on the line.

"Please put on your heavy winter coat before you go sledding," said my mom.

My mom wanted me to keep

______________. cool warm

I put on my coat ______________ I went sledding. before after

"Don't forget to bring your glasses, Tom! It will be hard to see the chalkboard if you don't wear them," reminded his dad.

Tom has ______________ eyesight.

good poor

Tom is ______________.

forgetful aware

Tom is going to ______________.

school basketball practice

Name ____________________

Where Do I Go?

Read the questions below. Then select words from the Word List to write on the lines.

Word List		
hospital	bookstore	bakery
	park	

My mom loves donuts. Dad and I wanted to surprise her with some. We stopped at the

____________________.

I love to read books! My mom said she would buy me a book at the

____________________.

I hurt my ankle at my basketball game. My coach took me to the

____________________.

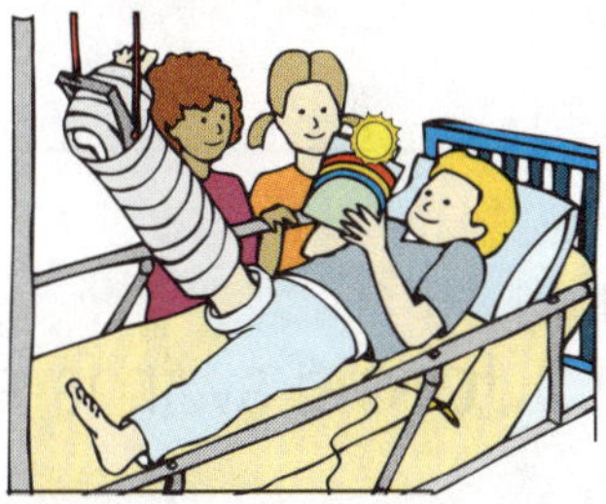

It was a warm summer day and my family went to the

____________________.

Help Hattie!

Name ______________________________

Help Hattie pick out birthday presents! Read the sentences about her friends. Then write words from the Word List on the lines. Draw a picture of each present inside the boxes.

Word List

music	airplane	goggles
crayons	journal	

Nancy loves to color pictures.

____

Ray wants to be a pilot.

____

Kristin loves to write.

____

Jared swims every week.

____

Chelsea is a great piano player.

____

Name ______________________________

What Will Happen Next?

Write what happens next:

____

____

What's Next?

Name ______________________________

Draw a picture of what will happen next in the boxes below:

Name ____________________

What Happens Next?

Read each paragraph. Predict what will happen and circle your answer choice.

David and Fran go the park. The friendly ice cream man is there selling ice cream cones. "Hi kids, would you two like an ice cream cone?" he asks.

Fran and David reach into their pockets, which are empty. "We don't have any money," says Fran. The ice cream man smiles at them and reaches into his freezer. Then he says...

A) Ice cream is bad for children.

B) Today it is my treat. Free ice cream for both of you!

C) I am sorry, maybe next time.

Draw a picture of what you think will happen:

Following Directions—Animal Riddles

Name ___________________________

Fill in the letters to name an animal that fits each description. Then draw the animal in the frames.

I wish I walked faster.

___ ___ ___ t l e

I like to eat nuts.

___ ___ ___ i r r ___ ___

I have a very long neck.

___ ___ ___ ___ f f e

I have black and white stripes.

___ ___ ___ n k

I have eight legs and spin webs.

s p ___ ___ ___ ___

Finding Mistakes—Tricky Triplets

In each row, circle the two that are the same.

Name ______________________________

Stop Making Sense!

Look at the picture. A lot of silly things are happening! Draw a circle around all the things that **do** make sense.

Name ____________________

Costume Jamboree!

Justin and his friends are dressed up for a costume party. Look at their pictures below and read the clues. Then write each child's name on the line below his or her picture. Color their costumes.

Costume clues:

- Justin and Jordan are pirates. Justin has a beard and Jordan has a mustache.
- Jackie is an animal trainer and wears pants and a neckerchief. She can make a dog jump through a hoop.
- Julie is a princess with blonde wavy hair and a bow.
- Jesse is a purple ghost and is standing next to Julie.

____________ ____________ ____________ ____________ ____________

Name ____________________

Story Mix-Up!

Here are some pictures from different stories. They are all mixed up.

One story is "Jack and the Beanstalk." Mark all of those pictures with a **J**. Another story is "The Three Little Pigs." Mark all of those pictures with a **P**. The third story is "Cinderella." Mark all of those pictures with a **C**.

Name ______________________________

Just for Fun!

Look at the workers below. Where would the best place be for each person to work: in the sky, on the ground, or in the water?

Put an **S** on each worker that would be in the sky. Put a **G** on each worker that would be on the ground. Put a **W** on each worker that would be in the water. Be careful! Some workers could be in more than one place.

Name ________________________________

What Can I Make?

Look at the pictures in each box below. Think about what you could make with those things. Then draw a picture of your idea.

Answers

Page 5
bright pretty
center plate
fast hop
silly dad

Page 6
scream ill
Synonyms and sentences will vary.

Page 7
tired, bag, pick, pull, cut, porch

Page 8
Pictures will vary but should portray the opposite of the first picture.

Page 9
pull: push
fast: slow
thin: fat
break: fix
harm: help
winter: summer
loser: winner

Page 10
light
right
low
quickly
shouted
child
weak
noisy

Page 11
can: A, B
band: A, B
cap: B, A
crow: B, A

Page 12
D E A
F B C

Page 13
A
B
A
B
A

Page 14
quiet
quite

freight
fright

loose
lose

Page 15
couch
coach

picture
pitcher

guest
guessed

Page 16
late – tired
broke – angry
tutu – silly

Page 17
cold wind, lack of heat – jacket
small islands – large
vitamins – good
very large, a lot – many

Page 18
yummy
tease
stop
lively
shined
smart

Page 19
tell
understand
little
petted
yelled

Page 21
Jumpin' Jack
Jumpin' Jack had two pointy white ears, a black body, and four white feet that looked like socks.
He shared his food and helped baby bunnies with their hops.
Answers will vary.

Page 22
Interview questions and answers will vary.

Page 23
Places will vary.

Page 24
It was very hot during the day and cold at night.

I would take summer clothes for during the day and warmer ones for night.

No, because the ground is too dry.

There are no trees to climb in the desert.

Page 25
The story takes place on Sunday.

The season is summer.

It is morning.

Page 26
Maps will vary.

Page 27
Answers will vary.

Page 28
Newspaper articles will vary but should use the information written on page 27.

Page 29
nonfiction

fiction

nonfiction

Page 30
fiction

nonfiction

Page 31
3 1
1 3
2 2

Page 32

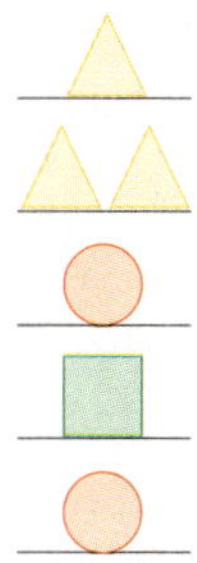

Page 33
CLIMB UP A TREE AND ACT LIKE A NUT.

A GARBAGE TRUCK

TO CATCH UP ON HIS SLEEP

Page 34
1. My cat was hungry.
2. I filled a bowl with cat food.
3. My cat was full and went to sleep.

1. My teacher gave us a list of spelling words.
2. I studied for my spelling test.
3. I got a gold star.

Page 35

bowl, spatula, mixer, paper towels, cupcake tin, spoon, cat, milk, girl

Chocolate Attack!

They aren't as clever or as interesting.

Page 36

Asleep for the Winter

Our New Fish

Spring Cleaning

Page 37

Titles will vary.

Page 38

no
yes
yes
no
yes
no
Sentences will vary.

Page 39

1. no
2. no
3. no
4. John and his mother made a fort.

Page 40

girl's baseball cap is turned differently

third flower has 8 petals

Page 41

Cow is a cashier; it's wearing a hat
elephant is in parrot cage
dogfish is not a real fish
mouse is in scuba gear in a fish tank
iguana has braces
the snail is not a dog and should not have a collar
boy in animal cage
gerbil in sneakers
"new kittens" sign points to puppies

Page 42

1. bears, whales, sea otters, moose

2. bug spray, raincoat

3. flamingos, platypuses, lions

Page 43

2. Sally has a lot to learn about caring for her new pet.

1. How to clean its cage

Page 44

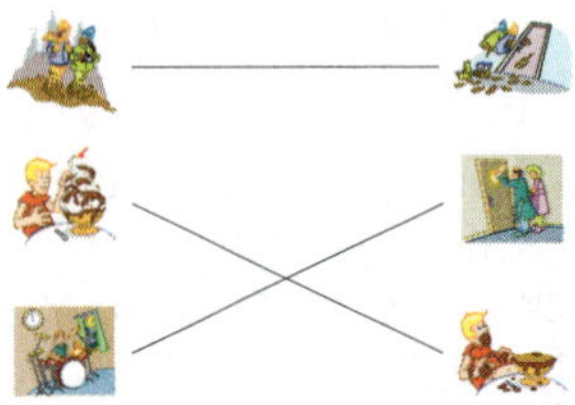

Page 45

Page 46

Page 47

Now they have room inside the garage to store Erin's bike.

Frank made the basketball team.

Page 48

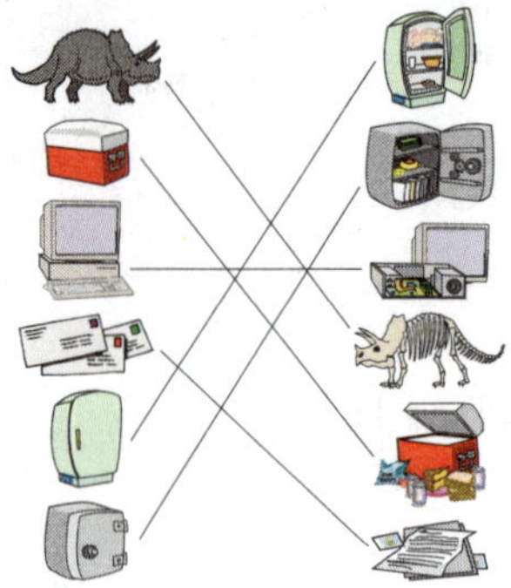

Page 49

Famous Actresses of the Stage, Amazing Animals of the Amazon, Abraham Lincoln's Life, Spend a Day With a Doctor!

Page 50

warm
before
poor
forgetful
school

Page 51

bakery
bookstore
hospital
park

Page 52

crayons
airplane
journal
goggles
music

Page 53

Answer will vary.

Page 54

Pictures will vary but should make sense given the first picture.

Page 55

Pictures will vary.

Page 56

turtle
squirrel
giraffe
skunk
spider
Children should draw pictures of each animal in the box opposite its name.

Page 57

first and second girl
first and third boy
second and third deer
first and second frog

Page 58

scuba divers, fish, seaweed, ocean, bubbles should be circled

Page 59

Justin Jesse Julie Jordan Jackie

Page 60

P	J	C
J	C	P
J	P	C

Page 61

trapeze artist – S
astronaut – S
cook – G
scuba diver – S
mail carrier – G
sailor – S
officer – G
fireman – S or G

Page 62

Pictures will vary.